Idries Shah was born in India in 1924 into an Afghan family
descended from Mohammed. He was brought up in the lore of the
dervishes and educated in the school established on traditional Sufi
principles by his grandfather, where he was provided with a thorough
background of classical Persian and Arabic and all forms of Sufi
psychological training, as well as a wide understanding of Western
languages and modes of thought. He has lived and travelled in many
countries and has published books on the development, diffusion and
interpretation of religious, philosophical and esoteric ideas in various
communities. His book, *The Sufis*, the most comprehensive account
of Sufism yet published, introduces readers to some aspects of
Mulla Nasrudin.

Also by Idries Shah in Picador

The Exploits of the Incomparable Mulla Nasrudin

Idries Shah

The pleasantries of the incredible Mulla Nasrudin

Drawings by Richard Williams and Errol le Cain

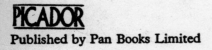
PICADOR
Published by Pan Books Limited

First published 1968 by Jonathan Cape Ltd
This edition published 1975 by Pan Books Ltd,
Cavaye Place, London SW10 9PG
Text and illustrations © Mulla Nasrudin Enterprises Ltd 1968

ISBN 0 330 24585 6

Made and printed in Great Britain by
Richard Clay (The Chaucer Press) Ltd, Bungay, Suffolk

Pidar natawanad, Pisar tamam kunad.
(If the Father cannot, the Son may bring it
to a conclusion.)

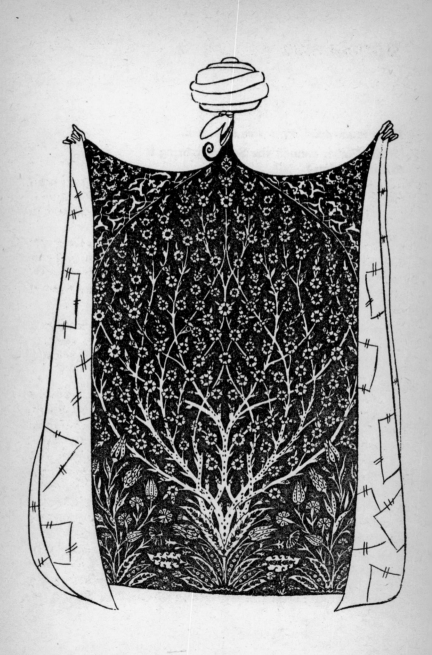

Introduction

hen one has heard several Nasrudin tales, they can have a compelling effect. There is a tradition, often recorded in the Middle East, which seeks to explain this.

It is related that Nasrudin, when a boy, had the strange power of keeping his schoolfellows' attention upon his stories. Their academic work suffered. The teacher, unable to prevent Nasrudin's magnetism working, was himself a sage who managed to modify it. He put this spell on the young man:

> From now, however wise you become, people will always laugh at you. From now, whenever *one* Nasrudin tale is told, people will feel compelled to tell them until at least seven have been recited.

It is quite curious how some people who are not immediately attracted to the Mulla can become addicts. The United States, the Soviet Union and Communist China are at this moment equally involved with Nasrudin, if with nothing else. The Coral Gables High-Energy Physics Conference report uses Mulla tales to illustrate scientific phenomena which cannot be put in the limitations of ordinary technical terms. In Soviet Central Asia a new Nasrudin film is in active production, as a cultural undertaking. Peking has published, in English as well as in Chinese, a folklore book containing stories about – Mulla Nasrudin.

Consistently with the Mulla's history, the widespread welcome of our version of *The Exploits* found a dissenter in – *Punch*. But if this could have been predicted from the Mulla's teachings, he would himself perhaps have been more diverted by the reaction of the academic experts. In Britain, orientalists have been saying that Nasrudin is not a Sufi teaching-figure. In Beirut and Karachi, the specialists' opinion to the contrary seems equally strong.

All this, of course, only serves to show that our Mulla does not fit into the current categories – and that there is nevertheless still a place for him.

According to the *Sayings of Mulla Nasrudin*:

Enjoy yourself, or try to learn – you will annoy someone. If you do not – you will annoy someone.

IDRIES SHAH
RICHARD WILLIAMS

The Reason

The Mulla went to see a rich man.
'Give me some money.'
'Why?'
'I want to buy ... an elephant.'
'If you have no money, you can't afford to keep an elephant.'
'I came here', said Nasrudin, 'to get money, not advice.'

Eating his money

ulla Nasrudin, as everyone knows, comes from a country where fruit is fruit, and meat is meat, and curry is never eaten.

One day he was plodding along a dusty Indian road, having newly descended from the high mountains of Kafiristan, when a great thirst overtook him. 'Soon', he said to himself, 'I must come across somewhere that good fruit is to be had.'

No sooner were the words formed in his brain than he rounded a corner and saw sitting in the shade of a tree a benevolent-looking man, with a basket in front of him.

Piled high in the basket were huge, shiny red fruits. 'This is what I need,' said Nasrudin. Taking two tiny coppers from the knot at the end of his turban, he handed them to the fruit-seller.

Without a word the man handed him the whole basket, for this kind of fruit is cheap in India, and people usually buy it in smaller amounts.

Nasrudin sat down in the place vacated by the fruiterer, and started to munch the fruits. Within a few seconds, his mouth was burning. Tears streamed down his cheeks, fire was in his throat. The Mulla went on eating.

An hour or two passed, and then an Afghan hillman came past. Nasrudin hailed him. 'Brother, these infidel fruits must come from the very mouth of Sheitan!'

'Fool!' said the hillman. 'Hast thou never heard of the chillis of Hindustan? Stop eating them at once, or death will surely claim a victim before the sun is down.'

'I cannot move from here', gasped the Mulla, 'until I have finished the whole basketful.'

'Madman! Those fruits belong in curry! Throw them away at once.'

'I am not eating fruit any more,' croaked Nasrudin, 'I am eating my money.'

The use of a light

'I can see in the dark,' boasted Nasrudin one day in the teahouse.

'If that is so, why do we sometimes see you carrying a light through the streets?'

'Only to prevent other people from colliding with me.'

the use of a light

'I can see in the dark'
boasted Nasrudin in the
teahouse one day
'If that is so, why do we
sometimes see you carrying
a light through the streets?'
'Only to prevent other people
from bumping into me.'

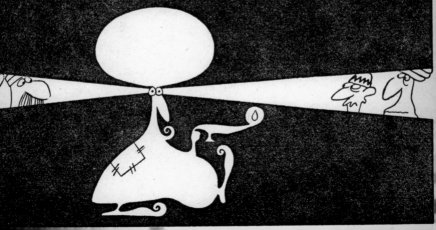

Why don't you?

Nasrudin went to the shop of a man who stocked all kinds of bits and pieces.

'Have you got nails?' he asked.

'Yes.'

'And leather, good leather?'

'Yes.'

'And twine?'

'Yes.'

'And dye?'

'Yes.'

'Then why, for Heaven's sake, don't you make a pair of boots?'

Prudence

The Mulla was invited to a wedding feast. The last time he had been to that house, someone had carried off his sandals. Now, instead of leaving them at the door, he stuffed them into the inner pocket of his coat.

'What book is that in your pocket?' his host asked him.

'He may be after my shoes,' thought Nasrudin; 'besides—I have a reputation as a learned man to keep up.' Aloud he said: 'The subject of the bulge which you see is "Prudence".'

'How interesting! Which bookshop did you get it from?'

'As a matter of fact, I got it from a shoemaker.'

Assumptions

'What is the meaning of fate, Mulla?'
  'Assumptions.'
  'In what way?'
'You assume things are going to go well, and they don't—that you call bad luck. You assume things are going to go badly and they don't—that you call good luck. You assume that certain things are going to happen or not happen—and you so lack intuition that you don't *know* what is going to happen. You assume that the future is unknown.

'When you are caught out—you call that Fate.'

Just suppose ...

The Mulla was walking down the village street deep in thought, when some urchins began to throw stones at him. He was taken by surprise, and besides he was not a big man.

'Don't do that, and I will tell you something of interest to you.'

'All right, what is it? But no philosophy.'

'The Emir is giving a free banquet to all comers.'

The children ran off towards the Emir's house as Nasrudin warmed to his theme, the delicacies and the delights of the entertainment ...

He looked up and saw them disappearing in the distance. Suddenly he tucked up his robes and started to sprint after them. 'I'd better go and see,' he panted to himself, 'because it *might* be true after all.'

Alternate crop

The Mulla went to the barber who shaved him with a blunt razor and a clumsy hand. Every time he drew blood, the barber stuck a wisp of cotton on the nick, to stop the bleeding. This continued for some time, until one side of Nasrudin's face was thickly dotted with cotton-wool.

As the barber was about to shave the other cheek, the Mulla suddenly caught sight of himself in the mirror and jumped up.

'That is enough, thank you, brother! I have decided to grow cotton on one side and barley on the other!'

Tit for tat

asrudin went into a shop to buy a pair of trousers.
Then he changed his mind and chose a cloak instead, at the same price.

Picking up the cloak he left the shop.

'You have not paid,' shouted the merchant.

'I left you the trousers, which were of the same value as the
cloak.'

'But you did not pay for the trousers either.'

'Of *course* not,' said the Mulla—'why should I pay for something that I did not want to buy?'

Whose servant am I?

ulla Nasrudin had become a favourite at Court. He used his position to show up the methods of courtiers.

One day the King was exceptionally hungry. Some aubergines had been so deliciously cooked that he told the palace chef to serve them every day.

'Are they not the best vegetables in the world, Mulla?' he asked Nasrudin.

'The very best, Majesty.'

Five days later, when the aubergines had been served for the tenth meal in succession, the King roared: 'Take these things away! I HATE them!'

'They are the worst vegetables in the world, Majesty,' agreed Nasrudin.

'But Mulla, less than a week ago you said that they were the very best.'

'I did. But I am the servant of the King, not of the vegetable.'

Inscrutable Fate

asrudin was walking along an alleyway when a man fell from a roof and landed on his neck. The man was unhurt; the Mulla was taken to hospital.

Some disciples went to visit him. 'What wisdom do you see in this happening, Mulla?'

'Avoid any belief in the inevitability of cause and effect! *He* falls off the roof—but *my* neck is broken! Shun reliance upon theoretical questions such as: "If a man falls off a roof, will his neck be broken?"'

The Answer

'There is nothing without an answer,' said a monk as he entered the teahouse where Nasrudin and his friends sat.

'Yet I have been challenged by a scholar with an unanswerable question,' observed the Mulla.

'Would that I had been there! Tell it to me, and I shall answer it.'

'Very well. He said: "Why are you stealing into my house through a window by night?"'

Idiots

Carrying home a load of delicate glassware, Mulla Nasrudin dropped it in the street. Everything was smashed.

A crowd gathered.

'What's the matter with you, idiots?' howled the Mulla. 'Haven't you ever seen a fool before?'

If Allah wills it

Nasrudin had saved up to buy a new shirt. He went to a tailor's shop, full of excitement. The tailor measured him and said: 'Come back in a week, and – if Allah wills – your shirt will be ready.'

The Mulla contained himself for a week and then went back to the shop.

'There has been a delay. But – if Allah wills – your shirt will be ready tomorrow.'

The following day Nasrudin returned. 'I am sorry,' said the tailor, 'but it is not quite finished. Try tomorrow, and – if Allah wills – it will be ready.'

'How long will it take', asked the exasperated Nasrudin, 'if you leave Allah out of it?'

A great thought

ne day Nasrudin asked his wife to cook *halwa*, a rich sweetmeat, and gave her all the ingredients. She made a large quantity, and the Mulla ate nearly all of it.

That night when they were in bed, he woke her up.

'I have just had a remarkable thought.'

'What is it?'

'Bring me the rest of the halwa, and I will tell you.'

She got up and brought him the halwa, which he ate. 'Now', she said, 'I shall not be able to sleep until you tell me the thought.'

'The thought', said Nasrudin, 'was this: "Never go to sleep without finishing all the halwa which has been made during the day."'

The Exploit

In the teahouse, some soldiers were boasting about their recent campaign. The local inhabitants crowded eagerly around them to listen.

'And', one fearsome-looking warrior was saying, 'I took my double-edged sword and charged the enemy, scattering them to right and left like chaff. We carried the day.'

There was a gasp of applause.

'That reminds me', said Nasrudin, who had seen a few battles in his time, 'of the time when I cut off the leg of an enemy on the battlefield. Severed it right through.'

'You would have done better, sir,' replied the captain of the soldiers, 'to have cut off his head.'

'That would have been impossible,' said the Mulla. 'You see, someone else had already done that.'

The Hunt

The King, who enjoyed Nasrudin's company, sent for him one day to go hunting bears. Bears are dangerous. Nasrudin was terrified at the prospect, but could not get out of it.

When he arrived back at the village, someone asked him: 'How did the hunt go?'

'Marvellously.'

'How many bears did you kill?'

'None.'

'How many did you chase?'

'None.'

'How many did you see?'

'None.'

'How could it go "marvellously", then?'

'When you are hunting bears, "none" is more than enough.'

Both, Your Majesty!

Nasrudin was not sure about Court etiquette, and yet he was among the notables who would have to be received by the Sultan when he visited the locality. An equerry quickly briefed him. The King would ask him how long he had been living there, how long he had studied to become a Mulla, and whether he was happy about the taxation and spiritual welfare of the people.

He memorized his answers: but they started in another order.

'How long have you studied?'

'Thirty-five years.'

'How old are you, then?'

'Twelve years.'

'This is impossible! Which of us is mad?'

'Both, your Majesty.'

'You call me mad, like you?'

'Of course we are mad, but in a different way, your Majesty!'

Forgotten himself

asrudin called at a castle to collect for charity.

'Tell your master', he said to the doorkeeper, 'that Mulla Nasrudin is here and asks for money.'

The man went into the building, then came out again.

'I am afraid that my master is out,' he said.

'Let me give you a message for him, then,' said Nasrudin. 'Even though he has not contributed he can have this advice, free. Next time he goes out he should not leave his face at the window. Someone might steal it.'

Not so difficult

The Mulla's neighbour wanted to borrow his clothes-line.

'Sorry,' said Nasrudin, 'I am using it. Drying flour.'

'How on earth can you dry flour on a clothes-line?'

'It is less difficult than you think when you do not want to lend it.'

Obligation

The Mulla nearly fell into a pool. A man whom he knew slightly was near and saved him. Every time he met Nasrudin after that he would remind him of the service which he had performed.

When this had happened several times Nasrudin took him to the water, jumped in, stood with his head just above water and shouted: '*Now* I am as wet as I would have been if you had not saved me! Leave me alone.'

Fixed ideas

'How old are you, Mulla?'
    'Forty.'
    'But you said the same last time I asked you, two years ago!'
  'Yes, I always stand by what I have said.'

There is a different time-scale

asrudin went to a Turkish bath. As he was poorly dressed the attendants treated him in a casual manner, gave him only a scrap of soap and an old towel.

When he left, Nasrudin gave the two men a gold coin each. He had not complained, and they could not understand it. Could it be, they wondered, that if he had been better treated he would have given an even larger tip?

The following week the Mulla appeared again. This time, of course, he was looked after like a king. After being massaged, perfumed and treated with the utmost deference, he left the bath, handing each attendant the smallest possible copper coin.

'This', said Nasrudin, 'is for last time. The gold coins were for this time.'

Man bites dog – that's news

Nasrudin had been out of town on one of his long hikes. As he entered the village he saw the people hurrying, one and all, towards the market-place.

He asked a passer-by what was going on.

'Don't you know? A man has been on the pilgrimage to Mecca. This year there were a hundred thousand people there— and he is giving a lecture about it.'

'From the excitement', said Nasrudin, 'I had almost concluded that the pilgrimage had come to him—not the other way about.'

Just as well I came along

asrudin was walking past a well, when he had the impulse to look into it. It was night, and as he peered into the deep water, he saw the Moon's reflection there.

'I must save the Moon!' the Mulla thought. 'Otherwise she will never wane, and the fasting month of Ramadan will never come to an end.'

He found a rope, threw it in and called down: 'Hold tight; keep bright; succour is at hand!'

The rope caught in a rock inside the well, and Nasrudin heaved as hard as he could. Straining back, he suddenly felt the rope give as it came loose, and he was thrown on his back. As he lay there, panting, he saw the Moon riding in the sky above.

'Glad to be of service,' said Nasrudin. 'Just as well I came along, wasn't it?'

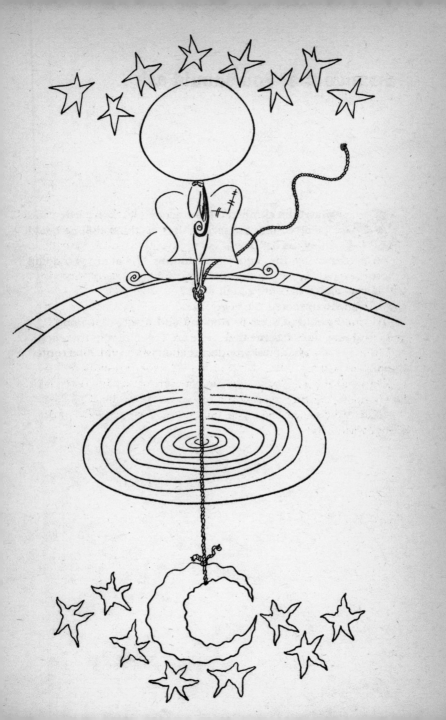

Strange that you should ask ...

asrudin climbed into someone's kitchen garden and started filling a sack with everything that he could lay his hands on.

A gardener saw him and came running. 'What are you doing here?'

'I was blown here by a high wind.'

'And who uprooted the vegetables?'

'I caught hold of them to stop myself being swept along.'

'And how does it come that there are vegetables in that sack?'

'That is just what *I* was wondering about when you interrupted me.'

Avoid entanglement

The ship seemed about to sink, and his fellow-passengers who had laughed at the Mulla's warnings that they should prepare their souls for the next world fell on their knees and cried out for help. In their lamentations they were promising what they would do if they were saved ...

'Steady, friends!' shouted the Mulla. 'Such prodigality with your worldly goods! Avoid entanglement, as you have in your lives so far. Trust me! I think I see land.'

How foolish can a man be?

The Mulla was found pouring wheat from the jars of his neighbours into his own, at the communal wheat-store. He was taken before the judge.

'I am a fool, I don't know their wheat from mine,' he stated.

'Then why did you not pour any wheat from your own jars into theirs?' demanded the judge.

'Ah, but I know *my* wheat from *theirs*—I am not such a fool as that!'

Cause and effect

One evening Nasrudin quarrelled with his wife and shouted at her so fiercely that she fled for refuge to a neighbouring house, where he followed her.

As it happened, a wedding feast was in progress, and the host and guests did all they could to calm him down, and vied with one another to make the couple reconciled, to eat and enjoy themselves.

The Mulla said to his wife: 'My dear, remind me to lose my temper more often—then life really *would* be worth living!'

That's why they bunged it up

asrudin was very thirsty and was happy when he saw by the roadside a water-pipe whose outlet was bunged with a piece of wood. Putting his open mouth near the stopper, he pulled. There was such a rush of water that he was knocked over.

'Oho!' roared the Mulla. 'That's why they blocked you up, is it? And you have not yet learned any sense!'

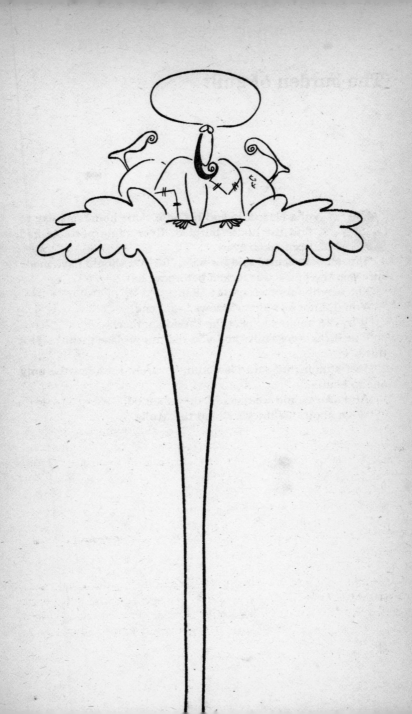

The burden of guilt

ulla Nasrudin and his wife came home one day to find the house burgled. Everything portable had been taken away.

'It is all your fault,' said his wife, 'for you should have made sure that the house was locked before we left.'

The neighbours took up the chant:

'You did not lock the windows,' said one.

'Why did you not expect this?' said another.

'The locks were faulty and you did not replace them,' said a third.

'Just a moment,' said Nasrudin, '—surely I am not the only one to blame?'

'And *who* should we blame?' they shouted.

'What about the thieves?' said the Mulla.

Description of the goods

Nasrudin lost a beautiful and costly turban.

'Are you not despondent, Mulla?' someone asked him.

'No, I am confident. You see, I have offered a reward of half a silver piece.'

'But the finder will surely never part with the turban, worth a hundred times as much, for such a reward.'

'I have already thought of that. I have announced that it was a dirty old turban, quite different from the *real* one.'

More useful

asrudin entered the teahouse and declaimed:
'The Moon is more useful than the Sun.'
'Why, Mulla?'
'We need the light more during the night than during the day.'

Which is my half?

Nasrudin and a friend were thirsty, and stopped at a café for a drink. They decided to share a glass of milk.

'You drink your half first,' said the friend, 'because I have some sugar here, just enough for one. I shall add this to my share of the milk and drink it.'

'Add it now,' said the Mulla, 'and I will drink only my half.'

'Certainly not. There is only enough sugar to sweeten half a glass of milk.'

Nasrudin went to the owner of the café, and came back with a large packet of salt.

'Good news, friend,' he said, 'I am drinking first, as agreed, and I want my milk with salt.'

Learn how to learn

The Mulla sent a small boy to get water from the well.

'Make sure you don't break the pot!' he shouted, and gave the child a clout.

'Mulla,' asked a spectator, 'why do you strike someone who hasn't done anything?'

'Because, you fool,' said the Mulla, 'it would be too late to punish him *after* he broke the pot, wouldn't it?'

Face the facts

Congratulations

'Congratulate me!' shouted Nasrudin to a neighbour. 'I am a father.'

'Congratulations! Is it a boy or a girl?'

'Yes! But how did you know?'

Too-obvious principles

'All should share equally in whatever is available,' a philosopher was announcing to an interested group at the teahouse.

'I am not sure that it would work,' said one doubter.

'But have you given it a chance?' demanded the idealist.

'I have!' shouted Nasrudin. 'I give my wife and my donkey exactly the same treatment. They get exactly what they want.'

'Excellent!' exclaimed the philosopher. 'Now tell the company what the results are, Mulla.'

'The result is a good donkey—and a bad wife.'

When you face things alone

'You may have lost your donkey, Mulla, but you don't have to grieve over it more than you did about the loss of your first wife.'

'Ah, but if you remember, when I lost my wife, all you villagers said: "We'll find you someone else." So far, nobody has offered to replace my donkey.'

The roles of Man

'Brother,' said Mulla Nasrudin to a neighbour, 'I am collecting to pay the debt of a poor man who cannot meet his obligations.'

'Very laudable,' said the other, and gave him a coin. 'Who is this person?'

'Me,' said Nasrudin, as he hurried away.

A few weeks later he was at the door again.

'I suppose you are calling about a debt,' said the now-cynical neighbour.

'I am.'

'I suppose someone can't pay a debt, and you want a contribution?'

'That is so.'

'I suppose it is *you* who owe the money?'

'Not this time.'

'Well, I am glad to hear it. Take this contribution.'

Nasrudin pocketed the money.

'Just one thing, Mulla. What prompts your humanitarian sentiments in this particular case?'

'Ah, you see ... I am the *creditor*!'

Dry in the rain

A man invited Nasrudin to go hunting with him, but mounted him on a horse which was too slow. The Mulla said nothing. Soon the hunt outpaced him and was out of sight. It began to rain heavily, and there was no shelter. All the members of the hunt got soaked through. Nasrudin, however, as soon as the rain started, took off all his clothes and folded them. Then he sat down on the pile. As soon as the rain stopped, he dressed himself and went back to his host's house for lunch. Nobody could work out why he was dry. With all the speed of their horses they had not been able to reach shelter on that plain.

'It was the horse you gave me,' said Nasrudin.

The next day he was given a fast horse and his host took the slow one. Rain fell again. The horse was so slow that the host got wetter than ever, riding at a snail's pace to his house. Nasrudin carried out the same procedure as before.

When he got back to the house he was dry.

'It is all your fault!' shouted his host. 'You made me ride this terrible horse.'

'Perhaps', said Nasrudin, 'you did not contribute anything of your own to the problem of keeping dry?'

What is real evidence?

 neighbour called on Nasrudin.

'Mulla, I want to borrow your donkey.'

'I am sorry,' said the Mulla, 'but I have already lent it out.'

As soon as he had spoken, the donkey brayed. The sound came from Nasrudin's stable.

'But Mulla, I can hear the donkey, in there!'

As he shut the door in the man's face, Nasrudin said, with dignity: 'A man who believes the word of a donkey in preference to my word does not deserve to be lent anything.'

Behind the obvious

Every Friday morning, Nasrudin arrived in a market town with an excellent donkey, which he sold.

The price which he asked was always very small; far below the value of the animal.

One day a rich donkey-merchant approached him.

'I cannot understand how you do it, Nasrudin. I sell donkeys at the lowest possible price. My servants force farmers to give me fodder free. My slaves look after my donkeys without wages. And yet I cannot match your prices.'

'Quite simple,' said Nasrudin. 'You steal fodder and labour. I merely steal donkeys.'

Objectivity

A neighbour came to Nasrudin for an interpretation on a point of law.

'My cow was gored by your bull. Do I get any compensation?'

'Certainly not. How can a man be held responsible for what an animal does?'

'Just a moment,' said the crafty villager. 'I am afraid I got the question back to front. What actually happened was that *my* bull gored *your* cow.'

'Ah,' said the Mulla, 'this is more involved. I shall have to look up the book of precedents, for there may be other factors involved which are relevant and which could alter the case.'

Nobody complains ...

Hamza, the homespun philosopher who peddled truisms in the teahouse, was droning on: 'How strange is humanity! To think that man is never satisfied! When it is winter, it is too cold for him. In summer, he complains of the heat!'

The others present nodded their heads sagely, for they believed that by so doing they partook of the essence of this wisdom.

Nasrudin looked up from his abstraction. 'Have you not noticed that nobody ever complains about the spring?'

How far can you usefully be from the truth?

Nasrudin saw some tasty-looking ducks playing in a pool. When he tried to catch them they flew away. He put some bread in the water and started to eat it.

Some people asked him what he was doing.

'I am eating duck soup,' said the Mulla.

I believe you are right!

The Mulla was made a magistrate. During his first case the plaintiff argued so persuasively that he exclaimed:

'I believe that you are right!'

The clerk of the Court begged him to restrain himself, for the defendant had not been heard yet.

Nasrudin was so carried away by the eloquence of the defendant that he cried out as soon as the man had finished his evidence:

'I believe you are right!'

The clerk of the court could not allow this.

'Your honour, they cannot *both* be right.'

'I believe you are right!' said Nasrudin.

It appears to be thou!

Nasrudin, standing utterly absorbed in the market-square, was reciting an ode:

'O my beloved!
My whole inner being is so suffused with Thee
That whatever presents itself to my sight
Appears to be Thou!'

A wag shouted:
'And what if a fool should come into your range of vision?'
Without pausing, as if it were a refrain, the Mulla carried on:

' ... It appears to be *Thou*!'

Ladder for sale

Nasrudin scaled a wall, and pulled his ladder over into the garden on the other side.

The owner caught him, and asked what he was doing there.

'I ... have a ladder for sale,' improvised Nasrudin.

'Fool!' said the householder. 'A garden is no place to sell a ladder.'

'It is you who are the fool,' said the Mulla, 'for you did not know that a ladder may be sold absolutely anywhere.'

Why camels have no wings

'Daily', said Nasrudin to his wife, 'I become more amazed at the manner in which nature is organized; and the way in which everything upon this earth is in some way planned for the benefit of mankind.'

She asked for an example.

'Well, for instance, you note that camels have no wings, by the mercy of Providence.'

'How does that help us?'

'Don't you see? If they had wings they might roost on house-tops, and destroy the roofs, to say nothing of the noise and the nuisance of their chewing and spitting their cud.'

The gold, the cloak and the horse

'I cannot get a job,' said the Mulla, 'because I am already in the service of the All-Highest.'

'In that case,' said his wife, 'ask for your wages, because every employer must pay.'

Quite right, thought Nasrudin.

'I have not been paid simply because I have never asked,' he said aloud.

'Then you had better go and ask.'

Nasrudin went into the garden, knelt and cried out: 'O Allah, send me a hundred pieces of gold, for all my past services are worth at least that much in back pay.'

His neighbour, a moneylender, thought he would play a joke on Nasrudin. Taking a bag of a hundred gold pieces he threw it down from a window.

Nasrudin stood up with dignity and took the money to his wife. 'I am one of the saints,' he told her. 'Here are my arrears.'

She was very impressed.

Presently, made suspicious by the succession of delivery men carrying food, clothing and furniture into Nasrudin's house, the neighbour went to get his money back.

'You heard me calling for it, and now you are pretending it is yours,' said Nasrudin. 'You shall never have it.'

The neighbour said that he would take Nasrudin to the court of summary jurisdiction.

'I cannot go like this,' said Nasrudin. 'I have no suitable clothes, nor have I a horse. If we appear together the judge will be prejudiced in your favour by my mean appearance.'

The neighbour took off his own cloak and gave it to Nasrudin, then he mounted him on his own horse, and they went before the Cadi.

The plaintiff was heard first.

'What is your defence?' the magistrate asked Nasrudin.

'That my neighbour is insane.'

'What evidence have you, Mulla?'

'What better than from his own mouth? He thinks that everything belongs to him. If you ask him about my horse, or even my cloak, he will claim them, let alone my gold.'

'But they *are* mine!' roared the neighbour.

Case dismissed.

Give him time

asrudin used to sit on the terrace of a certain tea-house. One day a small boy ran past and knocked his hat off. The Mulla took no notice.

The same thing happened several days in succession. All the Mulla did was to pick up his hat and put it on again.

Someone asked Nasrudin why he did not catch and punish the boy, who was small enough; or ask someone else to do it.

'That's not the way this thing is working,' said Nasrudin.

One day soon afterwards, the Mulla was late in reaching the cafe. When he got there he saw that a fearsome-looking soldier was sitting in his place. At that moment the small boy appeared. Such was the force of his habit that he tipped off the soldier's fur cap. Without a word the soldier drew his sword and cut off the boy's head, then resumed his seat.

'You see what I mean?' said Nasrudin to the friend who had questioned his inaction.

The Yogi, the Priest and the Sufi

asrudin put on a Sufi robe and decided to make a pious journey. On his way he met a priest and a yogi, and they decided to team up together. When they got to a village the others asked him to seek donations while they carried out their devotions. Nasrudin collected some money and bought halwa with it.

He suggested that they divide the food, but the others, who were not yet hungry enough, said that it should be postponed until night. They continued on their way; and when night fell Nasrudin asked for the first portion 'because I was the means of getting the food'. The others disagreed: the priest on the grounds that he represented a properly organized hierarchical body, and should therefore have preference; the yogi because, he said, he ate only once in three days and should therefore have more.

Finally they decided to sleep. In the morning, the one who related the best dream should have first choice of the halwa.

In the morning the priest said: 'In my dreams I saw the founder of my religion, who made a sign of benediction, singling me out as especially blessed.'

The others were impressed, but the Yogi said: 'I dreamt that I visited Nirvana, and was utterly absorbed into nothing.'

They turned to the Mulla. 'I dreamt that I saw the Sufi teacher Khidr, who appears only to the most sanctified.

'He said: "Nasrudin, eat the halwa—now!" And, of course, I had to obey.'

Remembering

here is a game called 'I remember', which has been the cause of greater suffering than almost anything else. It illustrates how difficult it is to remember even a simple thing for any length of time.

Two people make a pact to practise 'I remember'. Thenceforward, every time one of them hands anything to the other, the recipient must say 'I remember!' when he accepts the object.

The first person to forget to say this phrase under these circumstances loses the game and pays a forfeit.

Nasrudin had an 'I remember' duel with his wife. The honours were even, and they almost lost their reason, passing objects back and forth, until neither could stand the pace much longer. The Mulla devised a plan. He went on a pilgrimage to Mecca.

When he came back several months later, armed with a gift to hand his wife, finally to win the game in the excitement of the reunion, she met him at the gate.

In her arms was a bundle. 'I am not going to take it,' said the Mulla to himself. But, as soon as he was within a few paces of her, she said: 'Here is your new son.'

The Mulla, overcome with joy, took the child into his arms— and forgot to say: 'I remember.'

Refutation of the Philosophers

number of philosophers had banded themselves together and were travelling from one country to another
engaging local sages in learned disputation. When they
arrived in Nasrudin's town, the local Governor sent for the
Mulla to confront them, for all the intellectuals whom he had
produced were regularly routed by these strangers.

Mulla Nasrudin presented himself. 'You had better first
speak to those who have faced the philosophers,' the Governor
told him, 'so that you can get some idea of their methods.'

'Not at all,' said the Mulla, 'the less I know about their methods
of thought the better, for I do not think like them, nor will I
become imprisoned by their artificialities.'

The contest was staged in a large hall, before an enormous
gathering from far and near.

The first philosopher stepped forward to start the disputation.

'What', he asked the Mulla, 'is the centre of the Earth?'

The Mulla pointed with his pen. 'The exact centre of the
Earth is the centre of the spot upon which my donkey, yonder,
has his foot.'

'How can you prove it?'

'On the contrary, you disprove it. Get a measuring tape!'

The second philosopher asked: 'How many stars are there in
the sky?'

Nasrudin immediately replied: 'Exactly the same number as
there are hairs in the coat of my donkey. Anyone who disbelieves
this is at liberty to count both.'

The third philosopher said: 'How many avenues of human
perception are there?'

'Not at all difficult,' said Nasrudin. 'There are exactly as many as there are hairs in your beard, and I will demonstrate them if you like, one by one, as I pluck those hairs for you.'

'They are also', he continued, 'equal to the number of hairs in the tail of my donkey.'

The philosophers consulted together, realized that their theoretical speculations were incapable of logical or quantitative proof. With one accord, they enrolled themselves as disciples of Nasrudin.

Ask me another

'According to the general opinion of the uninitiated,' mused Nasrudin, as he walked along the road, 'dervishes are mad. According to the sages, however, they are the true masters of the world. I would like to test one, and myself, to make sure.'

Then he saw a tall figure, robed like an Akldan dervish—reputed to be exceptionally enlightened men—coming towards him.

'Friend,' said the Mulla, 'I want to perform an experiment, to test your powers of psychic penetration, and also my sanity.'

'Proceed,' said the Akldan.

Nasrudin made a sudden sweeping motion with his arm, then clenched his fist. 'What have I in my hand?'

'A horse, chariot and driver,' said the Akldan immediately.

'That's no real test,'—Nasrudin was petulant—'because you saw me pick them up.'

The Reward

Nasrudin had some good news for the King, and after a great deal of difficulty managed to gain an audience—although by tradition every subject theoretically had the right of immediate access to the Court.

The King was pleased with what he had been told. 'Choose your own reward,' he said.

'Fifty lashes,' said Nasrudin.

Puzzled, the King ordered that Nasrudin be beaten.

When twenty-five strokes had been administered, Nasrudin called: 'Stop!'

'Now,' he said, 'bring in my partner, and give him the other half of the reward. The chamberlain, Your Majesty, would not allow me to see you unless I would swear to give him exactly half of anything that I got as a result of my good news.'

The high cost of learning

asrudin decided that he could benefit by learning something new.

He went to see a master musician. 'How much do you charge to teach lute-playing?'

'Three silver pieces for the first month; after that, one silver piece a month.'

'Excellent!' said Nasrudin. 'I shall begin with the second month.'

The spiritual teacher

A wizened sage, from beyond Ashsharq, a far-off Eastern land, had arrived in the village. His philosophical expositions were so abstruse and yet so tantalizing that the usual company in the teahouse soon became convinced that he could perhaps unveil for them the mysteries of life.

Nasrudin listened to him for a while. 'You know,' he said, 'I have had experiences something like yours on your travels. I, too, have been a wandering teacher.'

'Tell me something about it, if you must,' said the elder, somewhat ruffled at the interruption.

'Oh, yes, I must,' said the Mulla. He continued:

'For instance, there was the trip which I took through Kurdistan. I was welcomed everywhere I went. I stayed at one monastery after another, where the dervishes listened eagerly to me. I was given free lodging at caravanserais, free food at teahouses. Everywhere the people were impressed by me.'

The ancient monk was becoming impatient at all this personal publicity. 'Did nobody ever oppose anything you said, at any time?' he asked querulously.

'Oh, yes,' said Nasrudin. 'Once I was beaten up and put in the stocks, then driven out of a town.'

'Why was that?'

'Well, you see, the people there happened to understand Turkish, the language I was doing my teaching in.'

'What about the people who had welcomed you?'

'Oh, they were Kurds; they have a language of their own. I was safe so long as I was with *them*.'

Hot soup, cold hands

A man who had heard that Nasrudin was very wise, decided to make a journey to see him. 'I can learn something from such a sage as this,' he thought. 'And there must be method in his madness, if one can only find the constant factor which must run through it. I have, after all, studied long and visited many metaphysical schools. This will enable me to judge and to learn, where others have failed.'

Accordingly, he undertook the long and tiresome journey to Nasrudin's tiny house, perched on a mountain-ledge.

Looking in through the window, he saw Nasrudin huddled beside a feeble fire, blowing into his cupped hands. As soon as he was admitted, he asked the Mulla what he had been doing.

'Warming my hands with my breath,' Nasrudin told him. After that neither party started any conversation, and the Seeker wondered whether Nasrudin would vouchsafe any of his wisdom after all.

Presently Nasrudin's wife brought two bowls of broth. Nasrudin immediately started blowing upon the surface of the broth. 'I may now learn something,' said the Seeker to himself. Aloud he said, 'What are you doing, Teacher?'

'Blowing on my broth to cool it with my breath,' said the Mulla.

'The man is undoubtedly a fraud, and probably a liar,' said the visitor, inwardly. 'First he blows for hot, then he blows for cold. How can I believe anything he may say to me?'

And he went away.

'The time has not been wasted,' he told himself, as he made his way back along the mountain road, 'for I have at least established that Nasrudin is no teacher.'

A word for it

earing that a man wanted to learn the Kurdish language, Nasrudin offered to teach him. Nasrudin's own knowledge of Kurdish was limited to a few words.

'We shall start with the word for "Hot Soup",' said the Mulla. 'In Kurdish, this is Aash.'

'I don't quite understand, Mulla. How would you say "Cold Soup"?'

'You never say "Cold Soup". The Kurds like their soup hot.'

Science

A scientist and a logician had met Nasrudin and wrangled with him as they walked along a road. Nasrudin was hard-pressed. The scientist said: 'I cannot accept anything as existing unless I carry out a test, or unless I see it with my own eyes.' The logician said: 'I cannot attempt anything unless I have worked it out in theory beforehand.'

Suddenly Nasrudin knelt down and started to pour something into a lake beside the road.

'What are you doing?' they asked together.

'You know how yogurt multiplies when you put it into milk? Well, I am adding a little yogurt to this water.'

'But you can't make yogurt that way!'

'I know, I know ... but—just *supposing* it takes!'

A question is an answer

Aren't we all?

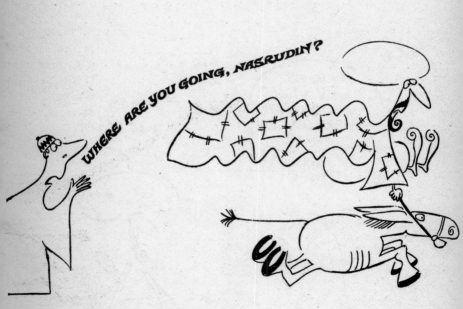

WHERE ARE YOU GOING, NASRUDIN?

I AM LOOKING FOR MY DONKEY!.....

The value of truth

f you want truth', Nasrudin told a group of Seekers who had come to hear his teachings, 'you will have to pay for it.'

'But why should you have to pay for something like truth?' asked one of the company.

'Have you not noticed', said Nasrudin, 'that it is the scarcity of a thing which determines its value?'

Take no chances

A theologian was ill. He had heard that Nasrudin was a mystic; and in his semi-delirium convinced himself that there might be something in all this, after all. So he sent for the Mulla.

'Prescribe a prayer which can ease me into the other world, Mulla,' he said, 'for you have a reputation of being in communication with another dimension.'

'Delighted,' said Nasrudin. 'Here you are: "God help me—Devil help me!"'

Forgetting his infirmity the divine sat bolt upright, scandalized.

'Mulla, you must be insane!'

'Not at all, my dear fellow. A man in your position cannot afford to take chances. When he sees two alternatives, he should try to provide for either of them working out.'

Guess what?

A wag met Nasrudin. In his pocket he had an egg. 'Tell me, Mulla; are you any good at guessing games?'

'Not bad,' said Nasrudin.

'Very well, then: tell me what I have in my pocket.'

'Give me a clue, then.'

'It is shaped like an egg, it is yellow and white inside, and it looks like an egg.'

'Some sort of a cake,' said Nasrudin.

The Merchant

 rich merchant spent some days in the village of Nasrudin. Although he was miserly, people were respectful towards him.

Nasrudin asked someone: 'Why do you salute him every time he passes? You never get a tip from him.'

'You don't understand: he is a merchant. That is something, isn't it? Besides, we feel he might give us something, one day.'

A week after the visitor had left, Nasrudin went to market. He bought a dozen water-melons at one stall, then sold them at the next. He made a loss on the transaction. Then he did the same again with something else. When he had been round most of the stall-holders, he went to the teahouse and airily ordered an expensive pink tea with whipped cream and flavoured with cardamoms.

Presently the teahouse began to fill with people, anxious to know what had happened to Nasrudin. Someone asked him: 'Mulla, why do you buy things and sell them again regardless of price?'

'How dare you ask me questions!' roared the Mulla. 'I am a merchant. That is something, isn't it? *And* I might give you something, one day!'

Don't run away with the idea. . .

asrudin was sedately riding his donkey along the road when it suddenly reared and he fell off. A group of small boys playing surrounded him and almost split their sides with laughter.

When they had wiped the tears from their eyes, Nasrudin sat up, and adjusted his turban with unruffled dignity.

'And what do you think you are laughing at?'

'Mulla,' they said, chortling at the memory, 'it was a wonderful sight! We were laughing at you falling off your donkey.'

'You have not taken into consideration', said Nasrudin, 'the possibility that I might have had a reason for falling.'

ZONK!

HA HA HA HA HA HA HA HA

WHAT ARE YOU LAUGHING AT?

WE ARE LAUGHING AT YOU FALLING OFF THE DONKEY!

DID IT EVER OCCUR TO YOU THAT I MIGHT HAVE HAD A *REASON* FOR FALLING?

The Chickens

ardly anyone could understand Nasrudin, because sometimes he snatched victory from defeat, sometimes things seemed to go astray because of his blundering. But there was a rumour that he was living on a different plane from others, and one day a young man decided to watch him, to see how he managed to survive at all, and whether anything could be learned from him.

He followed Nasrudin to a river bank, and saw him sit down under a tree. The Mulla suddenly stretched out his hand and a cake appeared in it which he ate. He did this three times. Then he put his hand out again, picked up a goblet and drank deeply.

The youth, unable to contain himself, rushed up to Nasrudin and caught hold of him. 'Tell me how you do these wonderful things, and I will do anything you ask,' he said.

'I will do that,' said Nasrudin, 'but first you have to get into the right state of mind. Then time and space have no meaning, and you can be reaching out to the Sultan's chamberlain to hand you sweetmeats. There is only one proviso.'

'I accept it!' shouted the young man.

'You will have to follow my way.'

'Tell me about it.'

'I can only tell you one thing at a time. Do you want the easy exercise, or the difficult one?'

'I will take the difficult one.'

'This is your first mistake. You have to start with the easy one. But now you cannot, for you have chosen. The difficult one is this: Make a hole in your fence so that your chickens can get into your neighbour's garden to peck—large enough for that. But it must also be so small that your neighbour's chickens cannot get into your own garden to feed themselves.'

The young man was never able to work this one out, and so he never became a disciple of Nasrudin. But when he told people about what Nasrudin could do, they thought that *he* was mad. 'This is a good start,' said Nasrudin; 'one day you will find a teacher.'

Prayer is better than sleep ...

As soon as he had intoned the Call to Prayer from his minaret, the Mulla was seen rushing away from the mosque.

Someone shouted: 'Where are you going, Nasrudin?'

The Mulla yelled back: 'That was the most penetrating call I have ever given. I'm going as far away as I can to see at what distance it can be heard.'

What is to be

A farmer asked Nasrudin whether his olives would bear in that year.

'They will bear,' said the Mulla.

'How do you know?'

'I just know, that is all.'

Later the same man saw Nasrudin trotting his donkey along a seashore, looking for driftwood.

'There is no wood here, Mulla, I have looked,' he called out.

Hours later the same man saw Nasrudin wending his way home, tired out, still without fuel.

'You are a man of perception, who can tell whether an olive tree will bear or not. Why can't you tell whether there is wood on a seashore?'

'I know what *must* be,' said Nasrudin, 'but I do not know what *may* be.'

The Logician

Nasrudin walked into a village and stood on a chair in the market-place.

When a crowd had collected, he declaimed:

'Know, O People, that the air here is similar to the air above my own village.'

'What makes you think so?' someone shouted.

'Because I can see the same number of stars here as I can when I am there.'

Once bitten

A man borrowed some money from Nasrudin. The Mulla thought that he would never get it back, but gave the money nevertheless.

Much to his surprise, the loan was promptly repaid. Nasrudin brooded.

Some time later the same man asked for the loan of a further sum, saying: 'You know my credit is good, I have repaid you in the past.'

'Not this time, you scoundrel!' roared Nasrudin. 'You deceived me the last time when I thought that you would not return the money. You won't get away with it a second time.'

Good news

n the East, people who bring good news are always rewarded, and this is considered a very important custom, never broken.

One day Mulla Nasrudin, delighted at the birth of a son, arrived in the market-place and started shouting: 'Gather around! Good news!'

'What is it, Mulla?'

Nasrudin waited until everyone was present, then cried: 'O people! Make a collection for the bringer of good news, news for every single one of you! This is the news! Your Mulla has been blessed with a son!'

The dog at his feet

ulla Nasrudin often wandered in graveyards, thinking about life and death. One day he was pursuing this uplifting activity when he saw a fierce-looking dog crouched near one of the tombs.

Outraged at this defilement, he took up a stick and waved it at the dog. But it merely growled, and seemed about to spring at him.

The Mulla was not one to expose himself to danger if it could be avoided. 'Sit there by all means,' he said reassuringly to the hound, 'for there is no objection so long as you crouch at the dead man's feet.'

Facts are facts

When the Mulla was made a Cadi [magistrate] he was faced with a difficult problem.

In an assault case the plaintiff said that the defendant had bitten his ear. The defence was that the plaintiff had bitten it himself.

'This is a clear conflict of evidence, because there are no witnesses,' said the Mulla. 'There is only one way to decide this. I therefore adjourn the Court for half an hour.'

He went into a room attached to the court-house, and spent the time trying to bite his own ear. Every time he tried he lost his balance and fell over, bruising his head.

When the Court reassembled, the Mulla said: 'Examine the head of the plaintiff. If it is bruised, he bit his own ear, and I find for the defendant. If, on the other hand, there is no bruise, the other man bit his ear, and that is assault.'

Not to be taken away

'I will instruct you in metaphysics,' said Nasrudin to a neighbour in whom he saw a spark of understanding, albeit a small one.

'I should be delighted,' said the man; 'come to my house any time and talk to me.'

Nasrudin realized that the man was thinking that mystical knowledge could be transmitted entirely by word of mouth. He said no more.

A few days later the neighbour called the Mulla from his roof. 'Nasrudin, I want your help to blow my fire, the charcoal is going out.'

'Certainly,' said Nasrudin. 'My breath is at your disposal—come over here and you can have as much of it as you can carry away.'

Not my business to know

Nasrudin's donkey was stolen.

He immediately went to the police.

'Mulla,' said the Chief of Police, 'this is serious. We will spare no effort to get your donkey back. After all, you are rather famous. Now begin at the beginning and tell me how it happened.'

'As I was not there when it happened, I can hardly tell you, can I?' said Nasrudin. 'Besides, it is not my business to know.'

Not as easy as it seems

A widow came to the Mulla's court and said: 'I am very poor. My young son eats a great deal of sugar: in fact he is addicted to it. This means that I cannot make ends meet. Would the Court forbid him to eat sugar, because I cannot myself enforce this request?'

'Madam,' said the Mulla, 'this problem is not as easy as it seems. Return in a week and the decision will be given, after I have examined the case more thoroughly.'

After a week the woman's name was again on the list of supplicants.

'I am sorry,' Nasrudin said to her when her turn came, 'there will be another adjournment of this very tricky case until next week.'

The same thing happened for the following fortnight. At length Nasrudin announced: 'The Court will now give its injunction. Call the lad.'

The young man was brought before the Mulla.

'Boy!' thundered the magistrate. 'You are forbidden to eat sugar, except for half an ounce a day.'

The woman now expressed her thanks to the Mulla, and begged leave to ask one question.

'Say on,' said Nasrudin.

'Your Worship, I am mystified as to why you did not forbid the boy to eat sugar at any of the earlier hearings.'

'Well,' said Nasrudin, 'I had to get myself out of the habit first, didn't I? How could I know that it would take so long?'

Repetitiousness

rofiting by the immense reputation which Sufis have as teachers of special insight, a group of robbers settled in an abandoned monastery on a highway, pretending to be Sufi dervishes.

Nasrudin and his small son were travelling on a long journey when they were espied by a lookout man among the robbers. They immediately started to carry out a rhythmic dance, with a great deal of noise.

As they approached, Nasrudin said to his son: 'Night will fall soon, and this seems to be a monastery of advanced dervishes. Let us seek their hospitality.'

The false dervishes welcomed them heartily, and even asked the Mulla to join their special exercises. These took the form of a rapid circular movement, with the repetition of phrases which were changed from time to time by the leader.

Presently Nasrudin was whirling with the best of them, taking up the repetitious cries and in a near-hysterical frame of mind. Now the leader of the 'dervishes' started to call: 'I give you my donkey! I give you my donkey!'

Obediently, Nasrudin echoed the refrain, and the tempo was increased until he fell unconscious.

When he awoke with the dawn, Nasrudin found the robbers—and the donkey—gone. 'I thought I left you in charge of the animal!' he roared at his son.

'Yes, Father. But when one of the dervishes came and took the donkey I ran to you, and you were shouting "I give you my donkey!" so often and in front of so many witnesses that I realized that you had given him away.'

Never miss a bargain

Nasrudin had so much against his donkey that the obvious thing to do was to sell it and get another one. So he went to the market-place, found the auctioneer, and gave him the donkey to sell.

When the animal came up for sale, the Mulla was standing by. 'And the next lot', shouted the auctioneer, 'is this superb, unequalled, wonderful donkey. Who will start the bidding at five gold pieces?'

'Only five for a donkey?' Nasrudin was impressed. So he started the bidding. As the price mounted higher and higher, with the auctioneer singing the praises of the donkey at every bid, Nasrudin became more and more anxious to buy. The bidding finally settled down to a duel between the Mulla and a farmer. At forty gold pieces it was knocked down to Nasrudin.

He paid the auctioneer his commission of one third, took his share of the money as the seller; then he took possession of the donkey as the buyer. The donkey was worth perhaps twenty gold pieces. So he was out of pocket: but he had bought a donkey of whose merits, as he now realized, he had been ignorant until they had been so glowingly portrayed by the town auctioneer.

'I never miss a bargain,' said Nasrudin to himself, as he walked home with his prize.

The omen that worked

A thief was stealing Nasrudin's cloak. By coincidence, at that very moment, his donkey started to bray.

Nasrudin was exultant, and started to shout: 'A marvellous omen! Good news! Safety follows an ass's braying!'

The thief was so alarmed at this noise that he dropped the cloak and fled.

The Change

From his childhood, Nasrudin was known as 'contrary'. His family had become so used to this habit of his that they always told him to do the opposite of what they wanted him to do.

On his fourteenth birthday, Nasrudin and his father were taking a donkey-load of flour to market. As dawn broke they were crossing a rickety rope-bridge, and the load began to slip.

'Quick, Nasrudin,' his father shouted, 'heave up the load on the left, otherwise the flour will be lost.'

Nasrudin immediately raised the left-hand sack on the donkey. The whole lot of flour was unbalanced as a result, and fell into the torrent below.

'Ridiculous fool!' said his father. 'Don't you always go by contraries? Did I not specify the left-hand load, meaning the right?'

'Yes, Father. But I am now fourteen years old. As from dawn today, I am considered to be a rational adult, and therefore I am complying with your orders.'

The value of a desire

asrudin had a buffalo whose horns were very wide apart. He had often thought that if he could mount between them, it would be just like sitting on a throne.

One day the animal sat down near him and he simply had to sit between the horns. He could not resist the temptation. The buffalo almost immediately stood up and tossed him.

His wife, finding him lying on the ground stunned, began to cry.

'Weep not!' said the Mulla, as he came round. 'I have had my suffering, but at least I have also attained my desire.'

When to worry

Nasrudin's donkey was lost. Everyone helped him to search the neighbourhood.

Someone said: 'You don't seem at all worried. You realize, do you not, that your donkey may never be found?'

Nasrudin said: 'You see that hill, yonder? Nobody has looked there yet. If they don't find it there, *then* I'll start worrying.'

Or else ...

Nasrudin went through the village, shouting: 'I have lost my saddlebag. Just find it', he continued in a thunderous voice, 'or else ... '

Alarmed, people went in all directions to look for the bag. Eventually it turned up.

'What would you have done, Mulla,' someone asked, 'if we had not found it?'

'I would have made myself another one out of some material which I have in my workshop.'

How long is too long?

man wanted to dock the tail of a horse. He asked the Mulla how long he should make it.

'It makes little difference,' said Nasrudin, 'because irrespective of what you do, opinions will differ; even your own opinion from time to time. Too long—no, too short ... '

Anachronism

'Why are you sitting at the crossroads, Mulla?'
'One day something will happen here, and a crowd will gather. When that comes about, I may not be able to get close enough—so I'm putting in my time now.'

No time to waste

Nasrudin ran to an appointment in a near-by town, stark naked. People asked him why.

'I was in such a hurry to get dressed that I forgot my clothes.'

Altruism

gain and again Nasrudin tried to tie a turban out of a piece of material which he had been given, but it was too short. Eventually he took it to the market and gave it to an auctioneer to sell for him.

When the sale started, he heard the auctioneer praising the cloth to the skies, and the bidding rose and rose.

'I cannot stand to hear so many good things said about a wretched piece of cloth which has caused me so much trouble,' thought the Mulla. 'Am I to conceal the shortcomings of such an unworthy thing?'

So he stole up to the man who had made the last bid and whispered to him: 'That muslin is hardly worth buying for a turban: it is a short length.'

Perhaps there is a road up there

Some small boys planned to steal the Mulla's slippers and run away with them. They called him, and pointed to a tree: 'Nobody could climb that tree.'

'Any one of you could,' said Nasrudin, 'and I shall show you.'

Removing his slippers he tucked them into his belt and began to climb.

'Mulla,' they cried, 'you won't need your slippers in a tree.'

Nasrudin, who had sensed without knowing why that he should take his slippers with him, reproved them: 'Be prepared for every emergency. For all I know, I might find a road up there.'

The Announcement

Nasrudin stood up in the market-place and started to address the throng.

'O people! Do you want knowledge without difficulties, truth without falsehood, attainment without effort, progress without sacrifice?'

Very soon a large crowd gathered, everyone shouting: 'Yes, yes!'

'Excellent!' said the Mulla. 'I only wanted to know. You may rely upon me to tell you all about it if I ever discover any such thing.'

What is above and what is below ...

A headstrong grandee had obtained from the Sultan the rights of share-cropping on the land occupied by Nasrudin. When the Court clerk asked him what crop he wanted to share, he merely said: 'Just put in "whatever is above the ground".'

He presented himself at the Mulla's house with the order duly sealed. But that year Nasrudin had planted turnips, and the above-ground share did not amount to much.

The following year the townsman arrived for his share, having had specified on his order the 'whole crop below ground'. This year, however, the Mulla was growing wheat.

The Speculator

Nasrudin bought a large number of eggs and at once sold them at a price lower than the cost.

When asked why he did it he said: 'Surely you don't want me to be called a profiteer?'

Louder than an ox

Nasrudin stole a bullock, killed it and removed the skin.

The owner traced the crime to him, and started shouting and wailing.

'Strange,' said Nasrudin, 'how cause and effect operates. I kill an *animal*, and the *owner* behaves as if he is being flayed.'

I did not start it

asrudin went to a mosque and sat down. His shirt
was rather short and the man behind him pulled it
lower, thinking it looked unseemly.

Nasrudin immediately pulled on the shirt of the man in front
of him.

'What are you doing?' asked the man in front.

'Don't ask me. Ask the man behind—he started it.'

In the mosque

asrudin was sitting meditating in a mosque, at the end of a row of the faithful. Suddenly one, involuntarily, said: 'I wonder whether I have left the fire burning at home?'

His neighbour said: 'You have broken your silence and spoiled the prayer. Now you will have to say it again.'

'So have you', said the next man.

'Praise be to Allah', said Mulla Nasrudin aloud, 'that I have not broken silence.'

Eggs

A group of youths took eggs to a Turkish bath where Nasrudin was expected.

When he came into the steam-room where they were sitting, they said: 'Let us imagine that we are fowls, and see whether we can lay eggs. The one who fails shall pay the bath fee for all.'

Nasrudin agreed.

After a little cackling, each one took an egg from behind him and held it out. Then they asked Nasrudin for his contribution.

'Among so many hens', said Nasrudin, 'there will surely be *one* cock?'

Allah will provide

'Allah will provide,' said Nasrudin one day to a man who was complaining that someone had stolen some cash from his house.

The man expressed doubt.

Nasrudin took him to the mosque, and rolled on the ground, calling upon Allah to restore the man's twenty silver coins.

Annoyed by his presence, the congregation made a collection and the sum was handed to the surprised loser.

'You may not understand the means which operate in this world,' said the Mulla, 'but I trust that you understand the end when it is handed to you in such a concrete form.'

The School

One of the boys at the Mulla's school asked:
    'Which was the greatest achievement, that of the man who conquered an empire, the man who could have but did not, or the man who prevented another from doing so?'

'I don't know about any of that,' said the Mulla, 'but I do know a more difficult task than any of those.'

'What is that?'

'Trying to teach you to see things as they really are.'

Clairvoyance

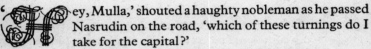ey, Mulla,' shouted a haughty nobleman as he passed Nasrudin on the road, 'which of these turnings do I take for the capital?'

'How did you know that I was a Mulla?' asked Nasrudin.

The other had merely used the word at random, but wanted to score off this bumpkin. 'I can read people's minds.'

'Very well,' said Nasrudin, making off, 'read the way to the capital, then.'

Invisible extension

Nasrudin saw a man selling a beautifully made sword in the market. 'How can a piece of steel be worth fifty gold pieces?' he asked.

The auctioneer saw that he was no connoisseur of art and said: 'This is a magical sword. In battle it stretches itself by several feet and outreaches the enemy.'

Within minutes the Mulla was back with a pair of firetongs. 'Sell these,' he told the auctioneer, 'and note that the reserve price is a hundred gold pieces.'

'I hardly think that you will get more than a few coppers for these,' said the man.

'Nonsense,' said the Mulla. 'They may appear to be ordinary enough tongs. But when my wife throws them at me, even from thirty feet, they leap across the gap, invisibly extended.'

Mistaken identity

ulla Nasrudin had had words with the Sheikh of a monastery where he was staying. One day a bag of rice was missing, and the chief ordered everyone to line up in the courtyard. Then he told them that the man who had stolen the rice had some grains of it in his beard.

'This is an old trick, to make the guilty party touch his beard,' thought the real thief, and he did not move.

'The chief is out to revenge himself upon me,' thought Nasrudin, 'and he is certain to have planted rice in my beard. I had better brush it off as inconspicuously as possible.'

He clawed his fingers through his beard: and found everyone looking at him.

'I knew that you would get me sooner or later,' said Nasrudin.

Deductive reasoning

'How old are you, Mulla?' someone asked.

'Three years older than my brother.'

'How do you know that?'

'Reasoning. Last year I heard my brother tell someone that I was two years older than him. A year has passed. That means that I am older by one year. I shall soon be old enough to be his grandfather.'

Let it be wheat

A neighbour asked Mulla Nasrudin to stand by him in a case of disputed possession of some grain.

'Did you see the transaction?' the judge asked Nasrudin.

'Yes, I distinctly saw the sacks of barley change hands.'

'But this case is concerned with sacks of *wheat*, not barley!'

'That is irrelevant. I am here to say that my friend is right. As a false witness surely I can say anything without its being held against me?'

The Genius

Nasrudin's little son was prattling away: 'Daddy, I remember the day when *you* were born.'

The Mulla turned triumphantly to his wife: 'There you are, Kerima—surely that proves that this child of mine is a genius?'

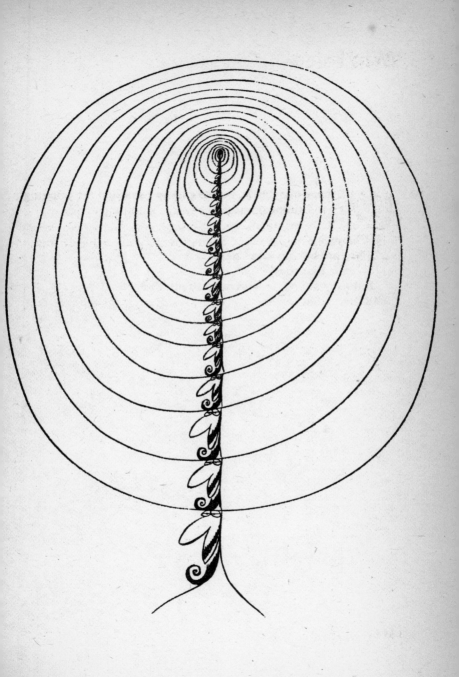

Why?

A local busybody, wanting to be rewarded for bringing good tidings, ran to the Mulla's house one day.

'Nasrudin! Good news!'

'What is it?'

'They are baking cakes next door!'

'What is that to *me?*'

'But they are going to give you some!'

'What is that to *you?*'

It is what he says that counts

A cruel neighbour wanted to borrow Nasrudin's donkey
'I'll have to ask his permission,' said the Mulla.
'All right, go and ask him.'
Nasrudin soon came back from the stable.

'I am sorry, he is endowed with prescience, and says that the future does not augur well for your relationship with him,' he told the man.

'What does he see in the future then?'

'I asked him. He simply said: "Long journeys and short meals, sore bones and scuffed knees." '

What will he find?

'There is a burglar downstairs,' said Nasrudin's wife one night.

'Not a sound,' whispered the Mulla. 'If he finds anything here, he will have to bring it into the house himself first. He may even leave something behind.'

Just for the asking

'I hear that you have some vinegar which is forty years old,' a neighbour said to Nasrudin. 'Will you give me some?'

'Certainly not,' said the Mulla. 'It would not be forty years old if I kept giving it away, would it?'

We come and we go

'Where do we come from and where do we go to, and what is it like?' thundered a wandering dervish.

'I don't know,' said Nasrudin; 'but it must be pretty terrible.'

A bystander asked him why.

'Observation shows me that when we arrive as babies we are crying. And many of us leave crying and reluctantly, too.'

The Karkorajami

'What is a Kar-kor-ajami?' someone asked Nasrudin's little boy, who had been talking about fairy-tale characters.

'Why, what its name means,' said the boy. 'It is a blind-deaf-and-dumb-walking-thing.'

'Yes,' interrupted the Mulla, 'and I taught it to be those things.'

The smell of a thought

asrudin was penniless, and sat huddled in a blanket while the wind howled outside. 'At least', he thought, 'the people next door will not smell cooking from my kitchen—so they can't send round to cadge some food.'

At that the thought of hot, aromatic soup came into his mind, and he savoured it mentally for several minutes.

There came a knocking on the door. 'Mother sent me', said the little daughter of his neighbour, 'to ask whether you had any soup to spare, hot, seasoned soup.'

'Heaven help us,' said Nasrudin, 'the neighbours even smell my thoughts.'

The Burglar

thief went into Nasrudin's house and carried away almost all the possessions of the Mulla to his own home. Nasrudin had been watching from the street. After a few minutes Nasrudin took up a blanket, followed him, went into his house, lay down, and pretended to go to sleep.

'Who are you, and what are you doing here?' asked the thief.

'Well,' said the Mulla, 'we were moving house, were we not?'

A matter of time, not place

man called, wanting to borrow a rope.
    'You cannot have it,' said Nasrudin.
    'Why not?'
'Because it is in use.'
'But I can see it just lying there, on the ground.'
'That's right: that's its use.'
'How long will it stay in use like that, Mulla?'
'Until such time as I feel that I want to lend it,' said Nasrudin.

All in my wife's name

Nasrudin was eating a huge roast chicken one day when a poor man passed by and said, peering through the window:

'Please give me some of that bird, for I am starving.'

'Willingly,' said Nasrudin. 'For my part I would give you all of it. But, unfortunately, it belongs to my wife.'

Waiting for the yeast to rise

Nasrudin's wife sent him to the river for water. She could not go, she explained, though it was woman's work, because she was waiting for the dough to rise.

The Mulla wandered to the riverside, reached in with the pot, and lost it in the water.

An hour later he was still sitting there, looking steadily into the water. Someone passing by asked him what he was doing.

'Waiting', he said, 'for the dough to rise.'

Even fire

The Mulla tried to get his fire going, but the embers would not produce a flame, no matter how he puffed on them.

Losing his temper he shouted: 'I'll bring my wife if you don't light!'—and puffed all the harder. The charcoal glowed more strongly, so he snatched up his wife's hat and put it on, to increase the effect. Suddenly he saw a flame.

Nasrudin smiled. 'Even fire is afraid of my wife!'

Later than you think

Deciding, for once, to fast for the thirty days of Ramadan, Nasrudin thought he would keep count by putting one stone for every day into a pot.

His little daughter, seeing her father do this, started to carry stones from all over the garden and put them in the pot, too. Nasrudin knew nothing of this.

A few days later some travellers passing by asked him how many days of the fasting month had passed. Nasrudin hurried to his pot and counted the stones. Then he came back and said:

'Forty-five.'

'But there are only thirty days in a month!'

'I do not exaggerate,' said the Mulla, with dignity, 'far to the contrary. The actual number is a hundred and fifty-three.'

On his own

The King had allowed a pet elephant loose near Nasrudin's village, and it was destroying the crops.

The people decided to go in a body to Tamerlane to protest. Nasrudin, because he had been known to amuse the King at times, was appointed leader of the delegation.

So overawed were they by the magnificence of the Court that the group pushed Nasrudin into the audience-chamber and fled.

'Yes,' said the King, 'what do you want, Nasrudin?'

'About your elephant, your Majesty ... ' stammered the Mulla. He saw that the King was in a bad temper that morning.

'Yes—what about my elephant?'

'We—that is, I, was thinking that it needed a mate.'

Limits of perception

Carrying some cocks to a certain place, Nasrudin thought he would let them out for a little, allowing them to walk part of the way. They started to wander in all directions, pecking at the earth.

'O fools!' shouted Nasrudin. 'You know when it is going to be sunrise; how is it that you cannot even understand where I am going?'

Which way round?

A man who had studied at many metaphysical schools came to Nasrudin. In order to show that he could be accepted for discipleship he described in detail where he had been and what he had studied.

'I hope that you will accept me, or at least tell me your ideas', he said, 'because I have spent so much of my time in studying at these schools.'

'Alas!' said Nasrudin, '*you* have studied the teachers and their teachings. What should have happened is that the teachers and the teachings should have studied *you*. Then we would have had something worthwhile.'

The milkman's horse

Nasrudin decided to sell firewood, and bought a milkman's horse cheaply to help him in his rounds. The horse knew his old round, and stopped after every few houses and neighed loudly. People came out with milkcans and reviled the Mulla when they found that he was only carrying firewood.

Finally, Nasrudin could stand it no longer, and he shook his fist at the horse, saying: 'Let us get this settled once and for all: Who is selling, you or me? You neigh to announce the firewood, and they attack me for not bringing the milk.'

What is it all for?

Nasrudin lay under a mulberry tree one hot summer's day, looking at some enormous water-melons which grew near by. His mind turned to higher things.

'How is it', he wondered, 'that an immense, impressive tree like this mulberry brings forth such puny little fruits? Look at the miserable, weakling creeper which produces such huge and delicious melons ... '

As he was pondering the paradox, a mulberry fell and landed on his shaven head.

'I see,' said Nasrudin. 'That is the reason, is it? I should have thought of that before.'

Pyramid expert

Nasrudin was sitting among the branches of a tree, sniffing the blossoms and sunning himself.

A traveller asked him what he was doing there.

'Climbing the Great Pyramid.'

'You are nowhere near a pyramid. And there are four ways up a pyramid: one by each face. That is a tree!'

'Yes!' said the Mulla. 'But it's much more fun like this, don't you think? Birds, blossoms, zephyrs, sunshine. I hardly think I could have done better.'

Where I sit

A t a gathering of divines, Nasrudin was seated right at the end of the room, farthest from the place of honour. Presently he began to tell jokes, and soon people were crowded around him, laughing and listening. Nobody was taking any notice of the greybeard who was giving a learned discourse. When he could no longer hear himself speak, the president of the assembly roared out:

'You must be silent! Nobody may talk unless he sits where the Chief sits.'

'I don't know how you see it,' said Nasrudin, 'but it strikes me that where I sit *is* where the Chief sits.'

Anyone can do it that way

An opinionated and small-minded cleric was lecturing the people in the teahouse where Nasrudin spent so much of his time.

As the hours went by, Nasrudin realized how this man's thoughts were running in patterns, how he was a victim of vanity and pride, how minor points of unrealistic intellectualism for its own sake were magnified by him and applied to every situation.

Subject after subject was discussed, and every time the intellectual cited books and precedents, false analogies and extraordinary presumptions without intuitive reality.

At length he produced a book which he had written, and Nasrudin stretched his hand forth to see it, because he was the only literate man present.

Holding it in front of his eyes, Nasrudin turned page after page, while the assembly looked on. After several minutes the itinerant cleric began to fidget. Then he could not contain himself any longer. 'You are holding my book upside down!' he screamed.

'I know,' said Nasrudin. 'Since it is one of the archetypes which seem to have produced *you*, it seems to be the only sensible thing to do, if one is to learn from it.'

Life and death

asrudin climbed a tree to saw through a branch. A passer-by who saw what he was doing cried: 'Look out! You are on the wrong side of the branch. You will fall with it.'

'Am I a fool that I should believe you; or are you a seer that you can tell me the future?' demanded the Mulla.

Soon afterwards, however, the branch gave way, and he fell to the ground. Nasrudin ran to catch up with the other man. 'Your prediction has been fulfilled! Tell me now, how shall I die?'

However much he tried, the other man could not now convince Nasrudin that he was not a seer. Ultimately he lost his temper and said: 'You might as well die now.'

As soon as he heard these words the Mulla fell down and lay still. His neighbours came and found him and put him in a coffin. As they were walking towards the cemetery, there was a dispute as to the shortest route. Nasrudin lost his patience. Raising his head from the coffin he said: 'When I was alive, I used to turn *left* here – that is the quickest way.'

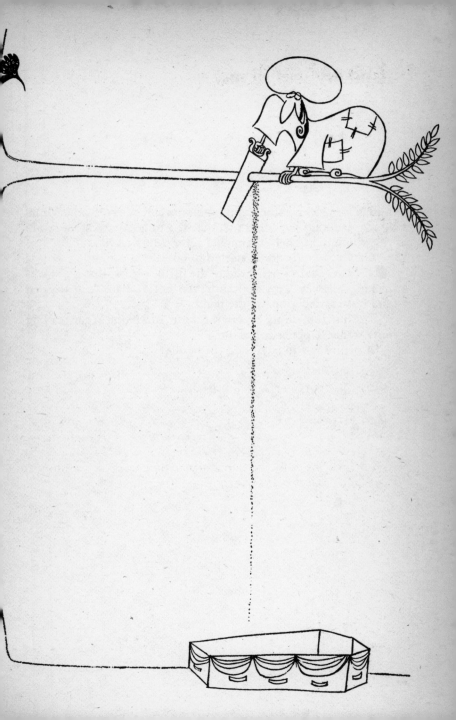

A penny less to pay

Sitting near some stepping-stones across a river, the Mulla saw that ten blind men wanted to cross the stream. He offered to help them over for a penny each.

They accepted and he started to take them across.

Nine were safely delivered to the further bank. But, as he was making his way with the tenth, the unfortunate man tripped and was carried away by the flood.

Sensing something amiss the nine survivors began calling out: 'What happened, Nasrudin?'

'A penny less to pay,' said the Mulla.

Why ask me?

asrudin was riding along one day when his donkey took fright at something in its path and started to bolt.

As he sped past them at an unaccustomed pace some country-men called out:

'Where are you going, O Nasrudin, so fast?'

'Don't ask me,' shouted the Mulla, 'ask my donkey!'

The Daughters

Nasrudin had two daughters. One was married to a farmer, the other to a brick-maker.

One day they both visited him.

The farmer's wife said: 'My husband has just finished sowing. If it rains, he will buy me a new dress.'

The other said: 'I hope that it does not. My husband has just made a huge number of bricks, ready for firing. If it does not rain, he will buy me a new dress.'

'One of you may be worth something,' said the Mulla, 'but I could not say which.'

All included

Nasrudin bought a handful of dates, and sat down to eat them. His wife noticed that he put each stone carefully in his pocket.

'Why don't you throw away the stones, like everyone else does?'

'Because when I bought the dates I asked the greengrocer if the price quoted for "dates" included "stones" as well. He said: "Yes, all included." So the stones are mine as well as the fruit. I can keep them, or throw them away.'

Why shouldn't they mourn?

Nasrudin used to breed chickens and sell them to the local butcher.

One day he was half-absorbed in the problems of his chicken-run when he noticed a man passing, dressed in mourning.

'Tell me,' said the Mulla, rushing to the fence, 'why are you wearing those clothes?'

'Because my parents are dead: this is how I mourn them.'

The next day passers-by saw each one of Nasrudin's chickens with a black ribbon around its neck.

'Mulla,' they cried, 'why are those chickens wearing black ribbons?'

'Their parents, as you may well imagine,' said the Mulla, 'are dead. Why shouldn't they mourn?'

Not worth keeping

Seeing something glittering in the gutter, Mulla Nasrudin ran to pick it up. It was a metal mirror.

Looking at it closely, he saw his face reflected in it.

'No wonder it was thrown away—nothing as ugly as this could possibly appeal to anyone. The fault is in me, for I picked it up without reasoning that it must be something unpleasant.'

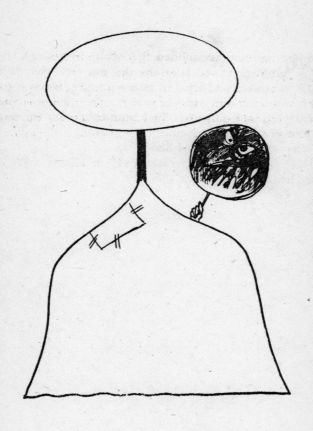

The Physician

A woman summoned the Mulla in his capacity as a physician, because she did not feel well. When he arrived and tried to take her pulse, she was too shy, and covered her arm with her sleeve.

Nasrudin took a handkerchief from his pocket and laid it on the sleeve.

'What are you doing, Mulla?'

'Didn't you know? A cotton pulse is always taken with a silken hand.'

Appetite

'I have been unable to eat anything for three days.'
    'Good heavens, Mulla—with your appetite? You must be very ill.'
'Not at all: nobody has asked me out to eat, that's all.'

The Secret

Nasrudin looked over a wall and saw a magnificent lawn, soft and green as finest velvet. He called to the gardener who was watering it:

'What is the secret of making a lawn like that?'

'No secret,' said the gardener. 'I don't mind telling you, if you climb down here.'

'Marvellous,' said the Mulla, scrambling down beside him. 'I'll make one for myself, and turn my whole garden into a lawn like this.'

'The method', said the gardener, 'is merely to plant a lawn, remove the weeds, and keep it flat and smooth, cutting the grass frequently.'

'I can do all that! How long does it take to get it into this condition?'

'About eight hundred years.'

'I like the outlook from my window–without grass–anyway,' said Nasrudin.

Maximum capacity

An ancient and valuable fragile Chinese vase had been found by the villagers. There was an argument in the teahouse as to its exact capacity.

During the wrangling, the Mulla entered. The people appealed to him for a ruling.

'Simple,' said Nasrudin. 'Bring the vase here, together with some sand.'

He had the vase filled with layer after layer of fine sand, packing it down with a mallet. Ultimately it burst.

'There you are,'—he turned to the company triumphantly—'the maximum capacity has been reached. All you have to do now is to remove one grain of sand, and you will have the precise amount needed to fill a container like this.'

Battle of the sexes

IN THE TEAHOUSE, PEOPLE WERE TALKING ABOUT THE RELATIVE NUMBERS OF THE SEXES "Throughout the world" SAID THE BAKER "men and women are equally balanced in numbers" "ON THE CONTRARY" SAID NASRUDIN "THERE ARE ABOUT TEN PER CENT MEN" "How do you make that out?" NINETY PER CENT DO WHAT THEIR WIVES TELL THEM TO DO

At the frontier

asrudin was carrying a basket of eggs across a frontier. The egg producers of the transborder country, anxious to preserve their rights, had petitioned the King. The King had decreed that no eggs were to be imported.

The customs officers on duty easily spotted Nasrudin, took him to their post, and started to interrogate him.

'The penalty for lying is death. What have you in that basket?'

'The smallest possible chickens.'

'That comes under livestock. We shall impound them', said the officer, locking them up in a cupboard, 'while we make inquiries. But have no fear, we shall feed them for you. That would be our responsibility.'

'These are special chickens,' said Nasrudin.

'How?'

'Well, you have heard of animals pining, getting old before their time, when deprived of the attention of their master?'

'Yes.'

'These chickens are so sensitive, and of such a special breed that if they are left alone for a moment, they become *young* before their time.'

'How young?'

'They can even become eggs again.'

Try anything once

asrudin was lurking near a tavern. He was penniless: and besides wine was forbidden to true believers.

The sultan's cup-bearer came out, carefully carrying a delicate flagon of wine.

They caught sight of one another at the same moment.

'Honourable Saki,' began the Mulla, 'give me ... '

'Give you *what*, Mulla?'

To ask for wine would be a direct admission that he drank it.

'Give me ... a piece of advice.'

'Very well. Go and read a book.'

Half to himself, Nasrudin muttered: 'Oh, no, that won't do.'

'Why not?'

'Oh ... er ... I tried that, once.'

Seven with one stroke

A soldier was back from the wars. The teahouse was agog.

'One day, on the Northern Frontiers, I slew no less than six infidels, all with red beards.'

There was a roar of applause.

'You can't cap that one, Mulla,' said a wag who had just tricked Nasrudin into swearing that he would tell the literal truth for the next twenty-four hours.

The Mulla drew himself up to his full height.

'I do not boast much, and I have sworn to tell the truth. Very well: know, all of you, that I have myself slain seven unbelievers, with a single stroke.'

He stalked out, as everyone looked at him with new respect, back to his room, where seven unbelieving beetles lay in the shadow of his fly-swatter.

Raw material

Everyone in the teahouse was criticizing Wali. He was generally admitted to be useless; and each person had something to say against him.

'That man', opined the tailor, whose words were usually considered weighty, 'is a cabbage.'

Everyone murmured his assent—except Nasrudin.

'Not so, Aga,' he said. 'You must be fair. A cabbage can be boiled and eaten. What could Wali be turned into?'

Catch your rabbit

People were talking about strange, sometimes mythical beasts, and someone in the teahouse told Nasrudin that there were monsters to be found even near his own village.

As he was on his way home, the Mulla saw a new animal. It had long ears, like a donkey, but it was brownish, furry and chewing. So preoccupied was it that Nasrudin was able to steal up to it and catch it by the ears. He had never seen anything like this before. It was, in fact, a rabbit.

He took it home and tied it in a sack, forbidding his wife to open it. Then he hurried back to the teahouse.

'I have found something', he announced gravely, 'which has ears like a donkey, munches like a camel, and is now in a sack in my house. There has never been an animal like this seen before.'

Immediately the teahouse emptied, and everyone ran to the Mulla's home to see this wonder.

Meanwhile, of course, his wife had opened the sack, unable to restrain her curiosity. The rabbit bounded out of the house and away. She could think of nothing better to do than put a stone in the sack instead, and tie it up again.

Soon the Mulla arrived with his friends clamouring to see the monster.

He opened the sack, and the stone fell out. There was a dead silence. Nasrudin recovered himself first.

'Friends! If you take seven of these stones, they will be found to weigh three-quarters of a pound.'

Pity the poor natives

asrudin was on one of his many teaching journeys, travelling through a rich country, heading for the capital.

As his donkey plodded along, he was more and more impressed by the orderliness and prosperity of the farms on each side of the road.

He reached the city on the first day of the new moon. Here it was the custom for people to go into the streets to see the crescent. Nasrudin knew nothing of this until he realized that everyone was pouring into the open and looking up at the moon.

'They may have a flourishing country,' said the Mulla to himself, 'but *we*, after all, have the moon almost all the time. She evidently appears here only when she is invisible to us.'

How far is far enough?

Nasrudin was at a loose end. His wife told him to go for a walk. He started up the road, and continued walking for two days.

Finally he met a man walking in the opposite direction.

'When you arrive at my house,' he said to him, 'go in and ask my wife if I have gone far enough, or if she says that I must walk farther.'

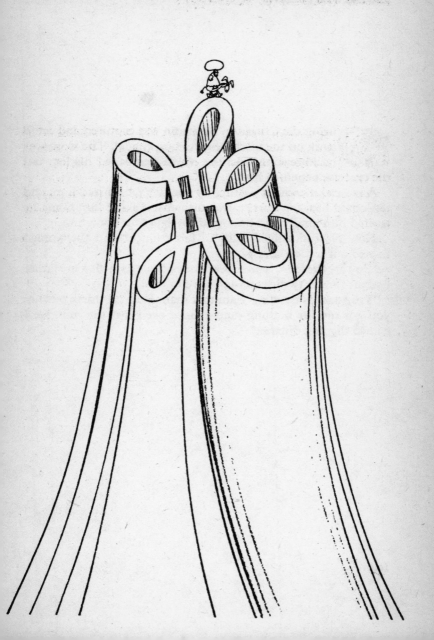

Economic law

During the Crusades, Nasrudin was captured and set to work on the ditch near Aleppo citadel. The work was backbreaking, and the Mulla bemoaned his lot: but the exercise benefited him.

A neutral merchant passing by one day recognized him, and ransomed him for thirty silver dirhams. Taking him home he treated him kindly and bestowed his daughter upon him.

Now Nasrudin lived a life of fair comfort, but the woman turned out to be a shrew.

'You are the man, remember,' she said one day, 'that my father bought for thirty dirhams and gave to me.'

'Yes,' said Nasrudin, 'I am that man. He paid thirty for me; you got me for nothing—and I have even lost the muscles I gained digging ditches.'

Private property

Trotting his donkey along a road one day, Nasrudin saw some beautiful flowers by the wayside. He dismounted to pick them, and when he returned with his posy found that someone had stolen his cloak from the back of the donkey.

'Very well,' said Nasrudin, 'I shall have your saddle instead. – Fair is fair.'

He got on the donkey and placed the saddle on his own back.

Tie up below!

The Mulla was aboard ship when a terrible storm blew up. All hands were ordered aloft to furl the sails and lash them to the masts.

Nasrudin ran to the captain, yelling:

'Fools! Anyone can see that the ship moves from below—and your men are trying to bind it up from above!'

Fire

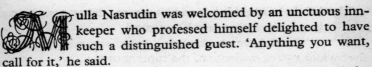ulla Nasrudin was welcomed by an unctuous inn-keeper who professed himself delighted to have such a distinguished guest. 'Anything you want, call for it,' he said.

During the night the Mulla was thirsty. He called out for water, but nobody stirred.

His throat was parched, and he felt as though there was a fire in his mouth.

'Fire! Fire!' he cried.

The whole caravanserai awakened, and presently the host was at his side with a pitcher of water. 'Where is the fire?'

Nasrudin pointed to his mouth. 'Here,' he said.

Instinct

'There are some things', said Nasrudin, 'that you positively know, inwardly, must be untrue.'

'Can I have an example?' asked someone who was always looking for evidence of the supernormal.

'Certainly. For instance, the other day when I was walking along, I overheard a rumour that I was dead.'

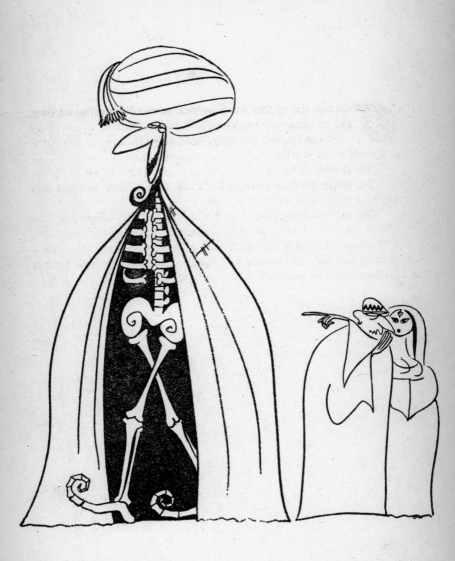

The question contains its answer

'Tell me the truth,' said Tamerlane to Nasrudin, as they sat in the steam-room of a Türkish bath.

'I always do, Majesty,' said the Mulla.

'What am I worth?'

'Five gold pieces.'

The King looked annoyed. 'This belt which secures my bathing-trunks is worth just that.'

'You are without value,' said the Mulla, 'and when you talk about "worth" I am forced to answer in terms of the question. If you are talking about money, I give you the exterior value— that of the belt. If you are talking about inner worth, it cannot be answered in words.'

Nosebags and donkeys

'Here is Nasrudin,' said someone in the teahouse during a philosophical discussion. 'Let's ask him a difficult question.'

'But all he knows about is donkeys,' said another.

'There is philosophy in donkeys,' said the Mulla, hearing the word as he entered.

'All right, Nasrudin,' said the baker, 'answer us this one: "What came first, donkeys or nosebags?"'

'Simple. Nosebags,' said the Mulla without hesitation.

'But that is ridiculous!'

'Prove it!'

'Well ... a donkey can recognize a nosebag, but a nosebag can't recognize a donkey.'

'I presume that you have the assurance of a nosebag', said Nasrudin, 'that it cannot recognize a donkey?'

The Mulla's dream

One night the Mulla woke his wife in a great hurry and said:
'Run, quickly, bring my glasses. I am having a wonderful dream, and more has been promised me by someone whom I have seen. I must have my glasses for this.'

The King spoke to me

asrudin returned to the village from the imperial capital, and the citizens gathered around him to hear what he had to say.

'I shall be brief,' said Nasrudin, 'and confine my remarks on this occasion simply to the statement that my greatest moment was when the King spoke to me.'

Overcome with wonder and staggered by the reflected glory, most of the people fell back, and went on their way to discuss this wonderful happening.

The least sophisticated peasant of all hung back, and asked: 'What did His Majesty say?'

'I was standing outside the palace when he came out, and he said to me, quite clearly, for anyone to hear: "Get out of my way!"'

The simpleton was satisfied. He had now, with his own ears, heard words which had actually been used by a King.

Nobody really knows

Suddenly realizing that he did not know who he was, Mulla Nasrudin rushed into the street, looking for someone who might recognize him.

The crowds were thick, but he was in a strange town, and he found no familiar face.

Suddenly he found himself in a carpenter's shop.

'What can I do for you?' asked the craftsman, stepping forward.

Nasrudin said nothing.

'Perhaps you would like something made from wood?'

'First things first,' said the Mulla. 'Now, did you see me come into your shop?'

'Yes, I did.'

'Good. Now, have you ever seen me in your life before?'

'Never in my life.'

'Then how do you know it is *me*?'

Truth

'What is truth?' a disciple asked Nasrudin.
'Something which I have never, at any time,
spoken—nor shall I.'

Last year's nests

'What are you doing in that tree, Mulla?'
　　　'Looking for eggs.'
　　　'But those are last year's nests!'
　'Well, if you were a bird, and wanted a safe place to lay, would you build a new nest, with everyone watching?'

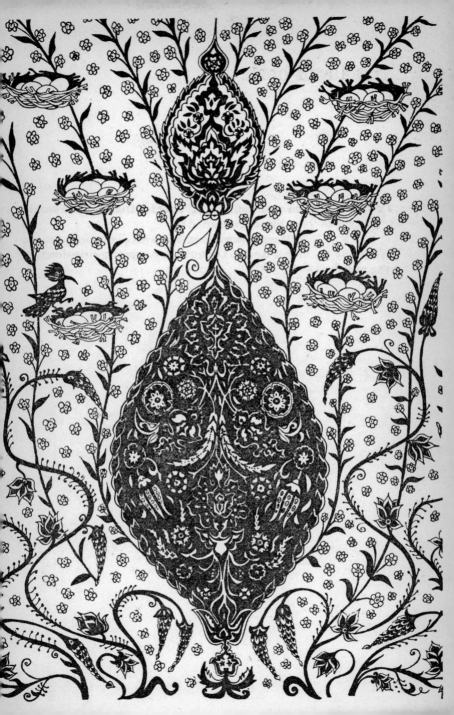

Head and heels

'When you die, Mulla,' asked a friend, 'how would you like to be buried?'

'Head downwards. If, as people believe, we are right way up in this world, I want to try being upside-down in the next.'

Just in case

asrudin was walking along the street enveloped in a dark-blue mourning-robe. Someone stopped him and asked: 'Why are you dressed like that, Mulla— has someone died?'

'Almost certainly,' said Mulla Nasrudin. 'It could have happened, you know, without my having been informed of it.'

Old graves for new

'When I die', said Nasrudin, 'have me buried in an old grave.'

'Why?' asked his relatives.

'Because when Munkir and Nakir, recording angels of good and bad actions, come, I will be able to wave them on, saying that this grave has been counted and entered for punishment already.'

Nasrudin's will

'The law prescribes that my dependents must receive certain fixed proportions of my possessions and money.

'I have nothing: let this be divided in accordance with the arithmetical formulae of the law.

'That which is left over is to be given to the poor.'

Incomplete

Mulla Nasrudin supervised the building of his own tomb.

At last, after one shortcoming after another had been righted, the mason came for his money.

'It is not right yet, builder.'

'Whatever more can be done with it?'

'We still have to supply the body.'

The Mulla's tomb

asrudin's tomb was fronted by an immense wooden door, barred and padlocked. Nobody could get into it, at least through the door. As his last joke, the Mulla decreed that the tomb should have no walls around it ...

The date inscribed on the tombstone was 386. Translating this into letters by substitution, a common device on Sufi tombs, we find the word SHWF. This is a form of the word for 'seeing', especially for 'making a person see'.

Perhaps it is for this reason that for many years the dust from the tomb was considered to be effective in curing eye troubles ...

Other titles in Picador

The Exploits of the Incomparable Mulla Nasrudin 50p
Idries Shah, with drawings by Richard Williams

A collection of stories about Nasrudin (an international folk hero of medieval origin but timeless appeal) which illustrate the philosophical teachings of the Sufis.

A Book of Dreams 60p
Peter Reich

The extraordinary account of life as friend, confidant and child of the brilliant but persecuted Wilhelm Reich. Peter, his son, shared with him his revolutionary concept of a world where dream and reality are virtually indistinguishable, and the sense of mission which set him and his followers apart from the rest of the human race.

Here Peter Reich writes vividly and movingly of the mysterious experiences he shared with his father: of the flying saucers, the cloudbusters and the FDA narks; and of the final tragic realization of his father's death which woke him up to the necessity of living out his life in an alien world.

Kentucky Ham 60p
William Burroughs Jr

'When I asked Clarence what the best way to cure a junkie was, he said, "Put in a new brain." And I think he was right . . .'

Kentucky Ham is the story of William Burroughs Jr's two battles against dope. The first, in the hopeless regimentation of the Lexington drug rehabilitation centre, he lost; but the second, which took place in the brutal freedom of an Alaskan fishing boat, he won . . .

'Brilliant . . . hilarious and moving by turns . . . Burroughs has a gift for vivid metaphors and offbeat insights that make his story something else in the inside-the-head-of-the-"head" category'
AMERICAN PUBLISHERS' WEEKLY

Grendel 50p
John Gardner

A fascinating, luminous reinterpretation of the Beowulf saga – from the monster's point of view. An outstanding novel; 'marvellous . . . absolutely marvellous, witty, intelligent, delightful, so totally a work of the imagination that it creates its own world' NEWSWEEK

The Blind Owl 40p
Sadegh Hedayat

The most important Persian work of literature written in this century. A young man, an old man and a beautiful young girl perform a ritual of passion, dreams and destruction.

One Flew Over the Cuckoo's Nest 60p
Ken Kesey

A contemporary American classic. Set in a mental hospital, this is the story of a struggle, against guilt and shame, for freedom and joy. One of the most influential books of our time.

The Existential Imagination 60p
edited by Frederick R. Karl and Leo Hamalian

An anthology of fiction, from de Sade to Sartre, which expresses existentialism. The authors include Kafka, Proust, Beckett, Brecht, Malraux, Dostoevsky and Pavese.

A Chinese Anthology 60p
edited by Raymond Van Over

A collection of Chinese folktales, fables and parables which, by any standard, can be termed definitive. It captures the elements which comprise the spirit of Chinese culture – intensity of imagination, wit and humour, human concern.

Rosshalde 50p
Hermann Hesse

The story of an artist's journey to self-discovery. By the Nobel Prizewinner who is perhaps the most influential novelist of our time.

Klingsor's Last Summer 50p
Hermann Hesse

The work which Hesse called 'my revolutionary book'. Written in the same period as *Siddhartha*, these novellas describe a time of immense emotional turmoil, of heightened pain, pleasure and perception in the lives of three characters.

Siddhartha 40p
Hermann Hesse

Hermann Hesse's greatest masterpiece. A profoundly moving love story and the account of a lifetime's quest for spiritual fulfilment.

If the War Goes On 50p
Hermann Hesse

The faith in salvation via the 'Inward Way', so familiar to readers of Hesse's fiction, is here expressed in his reflections on war and peace, on politics and the individual.

Knulp 50p
Hermann Hesse

The story of the loves and the wanderings of a vagabond whose role in life is to bring 'a little nostalgia for freedom' into the lives of ordinary men.